energy food

energy food

energy-giving food solutions to keep you fully charged throughout the day

Beverly le Blanc

This edition published in 2009
Love Food ® is an imprint of Parragon Books Ltd

Parragon
Queen Street House
4 Queen Street
Bath BA1 1HE, UK

Copyright © Parragon Books Ltd 2007

Love Food ® and the accompanying heart device is a trademark of Parragon Books Ltd

Internal design by Talking Design
Cover design by Sarah Edwards
Photography by Clive Streeter
Food styling by Angela Drake
Introduction and recipes written by Beverly le Blanc
Edited by Fiona Biggs

ISBN 978-1-4075-7868-2

Printed in Indonesia

NOTES FOR THE READER
This book uses imperial, metric, and U.S. cup measurements. Follow the same units of measurement throughout; do not mix imperial and metric. All spoon measurements are level: teaspoons are assumed to be 5 ml, and tablespoons are assumed to be 15 ml. Unless otherwise stated, milk is assumed to be lowfat, eggs and individual vegetables such as potatoes are medium, and pepper is freshly ground black pepper. Sufferers from liver disease and those with weakened immune systems should never eat raw fish. Likewise, pregnant women, nursing mothers, and young children should avoid eating raw fish, especially larger species such as swordfish and tuna, which tend to have high concentrations of mercury. Recipes using raw or very lightly cooked eggs should be avoided by infants, the elderly, pregnant women, convalescents, and anyone with a chronic condition. The times given are an approximate guide only. Preparation times differ according to the techniques used by different people and the cooking times may also vary from those given. Optional ingredients, variations, or serving suggestions have not been included in the calculations.

contents

introduction

If your zest for life and your energy seem to have disappeared, it is probably time to rethink your diet. The ancient Greek physician Hippocrates, remembered as the "father of medicine," had no doubt about the value of food in general wellbeing when he wrote "Let food be your medicine."

And two millennia later the advice is the same—eating a variety of energy-boosting foods throughout the day will not only leave you feeling more energetic, but will also help to keep you alert and better able to focus on whatever challenges you face, be they work pressures, schoolwork, or the general demands of running a busy household. *Energy Food* is a collection of quick-and-easy recipes that can help you feel more energized and make mealtimes a pleasure.

General tiredness and sluggishness are often caused by a lack of glucose in your bloodstream, or a low blood sugar level. To counter this and keep you on top form with enough energy to get you through the day and into the night, go for a balanced mix of lean proteins, unrefined starchy carbohydrates, and plenty of vegetables and fruit. That means choosing whole wheat pasta and breads over more refined white varieties; fresh and canned seafood; poultry, lean beef, pork and lamb; plenty of pulses; and whole grain breakfast cereals rather than sugar-laden, highly processed ones. The combination of ingredients makes positive eating for energy a real pleasure.

If you are in the habit of starting the day with a bowl of sugar-coated cornflakes, for example, you are no doubt familiar with the experience of leaving the house full of energy generated by the rush of sugar to your bloodstream, but then feeling "flat" several hours later, when you become sluggish and crave something sweet. At that point it's easy to reach for a cookie or slice of cake to revive yourself but, unfortunately, the feel-good factor won't last, and you'll soon be longing for something sweet again. This is what nutritionists and dieticians refer to as the "binge-and-crash" cycle.

Instead, let your diet give you the energy to keep you going until it's time for the next meal. If, for example, your breakfast is two slices of whole wheat toast or a whole grain cereal, such as Fruit & Nut Granola, the grains and oats will slowly release their energy into your bloodstream, which should leave you feeling satisfied and energized for longer. And, when you are in the mood for a quick pick-me-up, reach for something like an Orange Oat Bar, which will release its energy into your bloodstream slowly so you will feel better for longer.

A whole wheat Cheddar scone is another wise choice for a quick snack. Maintaining a constant blood sugar level throughout the day will prevent you feeling as if you are running out of steam.

If, however, your lifestyle doesn't suit sitting down for the traditional three meals a day, consider a grazing diet, where you eat small amounts of food every few hours. This eating pattern can also help keep your blood sugar levels constant so you don't feel tired and run down. But remember, you must keep your portion sizes small, or you will end up fighting excess weight, which will drain your energy levels even more.

However, as important as food is in optimizing your energy levels, don't forget that other aspects of your lifestyle are also important to your overall wellbeing. Regular exercise and sound sleep, for example, also influence how energetic you feel on a daily basis. But remember that energy requirements for an active, healthy life will be as individual as you are. You might have a friend who is able to function perfectly well and not feel run down with only five hours' sleep a night, but that doesn't mean that you can. And don't forget to take account of your age. As much as we would like it to be so, unfortunately, most of us simply cannot sustain the same level of physical activity when we are 40 as we could when we were 20. You should also make sure that you are eating enough food during the course of the day to fuel your body. Dieters often eat too little food to keep up their energy levels. An average healthy adult female should consume 1,900 calories a day, and a male should take in 2,755. It's up to you to make sure those calories work for you.

A Fresh Look at Carbs

Carbohydrates—the energy-providing substances found in food that come in the form of starches, fiber, and sugar—have had a bit of a bad press in recent years. Many people have cut bread, pasta, and potatoes, three major sources of carbohydrates, from their diets in favor of the low-carbohydrate meals advocated by the high-protein Atkins Diet. But carbohydrates are a good source of energy, and have an important role to play in keeping you active and healthy.

Carbohydrates are grouped into two categories—simple carbohydrates and complex carbohydrates. Simple carbohydrates, such as sugar, are quickly digested and absorbed into the bloodstream to provide almost instant energy. Complex carbohydrates, which come from starches and fiber, break down more slowly, giving you a longer-lasting source of energy.

The human body utilizes the energy from food in the form of glucose and glycogen. Glucose is most quickly absorbed into the bloodstream, giving you the familiar almost instant energy fix. Glycogen, on the other hand, is stored in your liver and muscles and then used by your body for more sustained energy. After your body has utilized the energy provided by glucose, the stored glycogen is converted into glucose to continue providing energy.

The high-carbohydrate Glycemic Diet is based on eating foods that are ranked low on the glycemic index (GI). The GI is a system for measuring how quickly carbohydrates are broken down during digestion and converted into glucose to raise your blood sugar levels and provide energy. The lower the GI rating of an ingredient, the more slowly its sugar is absorbed, helping to keep blood sugar levels constant. Many people choose the GI diet as a way of managing their weight and possibly reducing the risk of serious disease, such as Type II diabetes and coronary heart disease. Even without considering the long-term health benefits, incorporating low-GI foods into your meals is a useful way to avoid energy slumps.

Most foods have a high, medium or low GI rating. When you are planning energy-boosting meals, you should try to include ingredients with a low and medium GI rating, such as those included in this book. These include all pulses, such as chickpeas and lentils, and cannellini beans, flageolets, and kidney beans; fruit, such as apples, avocados, cherries, grapefruit, grapes, oranges, plums, peaches, and apricots; vegetables, such as eggplants, broccoli, zucchini, green beans, mushrooms, bell peppers, and sweet potatoes; and plenty of whole wheat foods, such as bread, pasta, and rice. This range of foods provides plenty of choice and variety, and you'll find these ingredients incorporated in the recipes in *Energy Food*.

Healthy eating guidelines recommend that at least half our daily calorie intake should come from carbohydrates and most of that should come from the complex carbohydrates. Eating low-GI foods to boost your energy, however, doesn't give you a license to eat unlimited quantities. Moderation, as with most things, is the key. On average, women should not eat more than 10 1/2 oz/ 300 g of carbohydrates a day and men should eat no more than 12 oz/350 g. Too much of a good thing can be counterproductive—a huge bowl of pasta, for example, will leave you feeling sluggish, so, again, keep portions of complex carbohydrates modest for maximum benefit.

Best Breakfasts

One easy way to add renewed vitality to your life is to eat breakfast every day. When you get up after sleep your body will have been fasting for at least six hours, probably longer. Your body has been performing millions of tiny functions, so it needs food to refuel. Running out of the door in the morning without eating something is like setting out on a car journey with an empty gas tank.

Numerous studies consistently confirm the beneficial aspects of eating breakfast. Apple & Spice Oatmeal, Buckwheat Crêpes, and Rice with Lentils are great for weekends and leisurely mornings. Even if you always find it a hectic rush to get out the door in the mornings, that isn't a reason to skip breakfast. Think simple: Fruit & Nut

Granola, Spiced Tea-Soaked Dried Fruit Salad, and Apple Muffins are all make-ahead breakfasts, requiring next to no time or effort in the mornings. Other quick-and-easy ideas include spreading peanut butter on whole wheat toast, wrapping a banana in a whole wheat pita, or a bowl of plain yogurt with nuts and dried fruit added. Or, quickly blend a batch of smoothies for the whole family to enjoy.

Tempting as it might be to pick up a croissant, donut, or muffin made with white flour on the way to the office or school, do yourself a favor and try some of the healthier options every morning for a week. You'll soon see how much better you feel as the morning ticks on.

And, if you think you can save calories by skipping breakfast, you're wrong. It has been confirmed in study after study that those who don't eat breakfast end up consuming more calories throughout the day, starting with the mid-morning snack when the body starts running down.

Food for Thought

Food fuels your brain, as well as your body. If you eat an energy-boosting diet you might find that you are experiencing other benefits, too, such as improved concentration and alertness. Researchers think this is because the brain has high glucose requirements but can store only small amounts. New studies indicate that boosting blood sugar levels after a night's fast improves mental function, including memory.

Simple, but Satisfying

A sudden, radical diet change might not be long lasting—and it can be difficult if you are cooking for others, not just yourself. Instead, try these simple ideas for boosting your energy levels:

- Keep a bowl of fruit on the counter for snacks. One of the numerous nutritional benefits of fruit is that it contains a host of B-complex vitamins, essential for the release of energy from food. Grapes, for example, are packed with the B vitamin that is involved in the first stage of the process that converts food to glucose.

- Add fresh mung bean sprouts to your favorite salads. They add crunch, as well as a burst of energy.

- Go for orange—sweet potatoes give you a steady energy supply that is missing from ordinary white potatoes. Baked Sweet Potatoes with Red Bell Pepper Hummus is a lunch idea that will keep you going through the afternoon.

- Snack on seeds—sunflower seeds, for example, contain B vitamins, as well as other nutrients. Keep a small bag with you during the day for a quick energy boost. Or, if you want more variety, take a bag of Trail Mix with you. (Again, moderation is the key here. Seeds are high in calories because of their fat content, but it is polyunsaturated fat, which is less "harmful" from a health perspective than the saturated fats found in many animal-based foods.)

- Go nuts for nuts—while nuts are also high in calories, the fat they contain is monounsaturated, so it's good to include a few in your daily diet.

- Great grains—grains are a wonderful source of complex carbohydrate and B vitamins, both of which help boost your energy levels. Whole grains are more beneficial than the processed variety. Use cooked whole grains or prepare Buckwheat-Tomato Bake as an alternative to rice with your favorite family meal. Tuna Pasta is a great way to introduce whole wheat pasta into mealtimes. Don't forget the Asian noodles, such as soba (buckwheat), which will add interest to stir-fries. They are quick and easy to use.

- Keep your pantry well stocked with cans of pulses, which are excellent sources of complex carbohydrates. They are ideal for adding to soups and salads. Dried pulses are very inexpensive, but require lengthy soaking before cooking, while the canned variety, although a little more costly, are ready to use. Dried or canned, they have the same nutritional value.

- Replace white rice with brown rice. You'll find numerous varieties, including long-grain and basmati, at your local health store.

breakfast boosters

It's often said that breakfast is the most important meal of the day and that's because your body needs to refuel after its night's fast. This chapter has plenty of quick ideas for kick-starting your body into action, as well as more leisurely ideas for relaxed weekend breakfasts when you have more time both to prepare and eat them.

makes about 20 servings

5$^{1}/_{2}$ oz/150 g jumbo
   rolled oats
5$^{1}/_{2}$ oz/150 g rolled
   wheat flakes
2$^{1}/_{2}$ oz/70 g rice flakes
2$^{1}/_{2}$ oz/70 g rye flakes
3$^{1}/_{2}$ oz/100 g raisins or
   golden raisins

3$^{1}/_{2}$ oz/100 g dried
   banana flakes
2 oz/55 g toasted
   hazelnuts
2 oz/55 g sunflower
   seeds or flax seeds
2 oz/55 g wheat germ
milk, for soaking

To serve
Greek-style yogurt
honey
milk

fruit & nut granola

There's no excuse for skipping breakfast with this tasty cereal—just put it in a
bowl and add milk. The slow-release energy will keep you going until lunchtime.

Put all the ingredients into a large jar with an airtight seal.
Seal the jar and shake to mix together.

Make sure that the ingredients are well distributed, then
pour over enough milk to cover the servings for the next
day and leave to soak overnight. In the morning, top the
granola with yogurt and honey and serve.

The dry granola will keep for at least a month in a well-
sealed jar. Just tip the jar upside down once in a while to
redistribute any ingredients that have sunk to the bottom.

serves 4

20 fl oz/600 ml milk or
water
1 tsp salt
4 oz/115 g medium rolled
oats
2 large apples

$\frac{1}{2}$ tsp ground mixed
spice
honey (optional), to serve

apple & spice oatmeal

A bowl of this old-fashioned favorite will help keep your blood sugar levels on an even keel throughout the morning.

Put the milk in a pan and bring to a boil. Add the salt and sprinkle in the oats, stirring constantly.

Reduce the heat to low and let the oats simmer for 10 minutes, stirring occasionally.

Meanwhile, halve, core, and grate the apples. When the porridge is creamy and much of the liquid has evaporated, stir in the grated apple and mixed spice. Spoon into bowls and drizzle with the honey, if using.

serves 8

6 oz/175 g dried apricots
3 1/2 oz/100 g dried apple
  rings, chopped
3 1/2 oz/100 g dried pears
3 1/2 oz/100 g golden
  raisins
3 1/2 oz/100 g dried
  cherries

5 lemon-ginger tea bags
several strips freshly
  pared lemon peel
2 cinnamon sticks
2 star anise

To serve
Greek-style yogurt
sliced banana (optional)
honey (optional)

spiced tea-soaked dried fruit salad

Keep your mornings easy with a bowl of this sweet and flavorsome kick-start in the fridge.

Put the dried fruit and the tea bags in a heatproof bowl and pour over enough boiling water to cover the fruit by 1 inch/2.5 cm. Set aside and let the fruit stew in the water for at least 2 hours, but ideally overnight, stirring occasionally.

Turn the fruit and any remaining soaking liquid, the lemon peel, cinnamon sticks, and star anise into a pan over medium heat. If necessary add extra water so the fruit is just covered and simmer for 10–20 minutes until the fruit is plump and soft.

Remove the pan from the heat and let the fruit and liquid cool. Transfer to an airtight container, seal, and store in the fridge for up to two weeks.

To serve, spoon the fruit into a bowl and top with yogurt. Add some sliced banana and honey, if using.

makes 10

9 oz/250 g buckwheat
    flour
3 oz/85 g all-purpose
    white flour
$^1/_2$ tsp salt
14 fl oz/400 ml milk
about 9 fl oz/250 ml
    water

about 2$^1/_2$ oz/70 g
    clarified butter, melted
$^1/_2$ tbsp sunflower oil
cherry tomatoes,
    to serve

Filling
7 oz/200 g creamy
    rindless goat cheese
4 large charbroiled red
    bell peppers in olive
    oil, drained and thinly
    sliced
salt and pepper

buckwheat crêpes

The buckwheat flour in these traditional French crêpes will give you a steady release of energy until lunchtime.

Sift the buckwheat flour, white flour, and salt into a large mixing bowl, then make a well in the center. Add half the milk and stir in the flour to make a thick, smooth paste-like batter. Beat until well blended, then gradually beat in the remaining milk. Cover the bowl with plastic wrap and set aside to rest for 45 minutes.

Uncover the batter and beat in 5 fl oz/150 ml water, then slowly beat in more water until the batter is the consistency of light cream. Add half the clarified butter and beat until well blended and not visible on the surface.

Heat a 9-inch/23-cm crêpe pan or skillet over medium–high heat until it is very hot. Spoon the oil into the pan and spread it over the surface. Reduce the heat to medium and continue heating the pan until a few drops of batter set on contact.

Rub the surface of the pan with clarified butter. Drop a small ladleful of batter in the center of the pan and immediately lift and tip the pan so the batter covers the bottom as thinly as possible. Cook the crêpe until it is golden brown and set on the bottom with holes starting to appear on the surface, then flip it over, using a metal palette knife, and cook until the other side is set.

Transfer the crêpe to a plate and keep warm. Repeat until all the batter is used.

Thinly slice the goat cheese. Arrange the crêpes on the counter in front of you, then divide the goat cheese and bell peppers among them. Turn the sides of each crêpe into the center, then fold in at the ends to make a square packet.

Reheat the pan. Rub with clarified butter, add the crêpes, folded side down, and cook for 90 seconds, then flip over and cook for an additional 30 seconds, or until the crêpes are hot and the filling warmed through. Serve hot, garnished with the cherry tomatoes.

8 large eggs
1 tbsp sunflower oil
2 tsp butter
1 large leek, trimmed,
 thinly sliced, rinsed,
 and patted dry

4 whole wheat muffins,
 split, toasted, and
 lightly buttered
salt and pepper

scrambled eggs with leeks

Serving these creamy eggs with whole wheat muffins, rather than white bread, will give you an energy boost that will keep you going for longer.

Put the eggs in a bowl and use a fork to whisk together until blended, then set aside.

Heat the oil with half the butter in a large skillet over a medium–high heat until frothy. Reduce the heat to medium, add the leeks, and stir around for about 5 minutes until wilted. Use a slotted spoon to remove the leeks from the skillet and set aside.

Add the remaining butter to the oil in the skillet. Season the eggs to taste with salt and pepper, then pour them into the skillet, reduce the heat to medium–low, and cook, stirring, for 1½ minutes, or until the eggs begin to set. Return the leeks to the skillet and stir into the eggs until the eggs have reached the desired consistency.

Spoon the egg and leek mixture over the hot muffins and serve.

serves 4–6

9 oz/250 g whole grain
  basmati rice
2¹/₂ oz/75 g red lentils
1¹/₂ tbsp sunflower oil
1 large onion, finely
  sliced
1 tsp cumin seeds
1 tsp ground coriander

pinch asafetida
30 fl oz/825 ml boiling
  water
1¹/₂ tsp salt
9 oz/250 g undyed
  smoked haddock
4 large hard-cooked
  eggs, chopped

2 large scallions, finely
  chopped
2 tbsp chopped fresh
  parsley, to garnish
whole wheat bread, to
  serve

rice with lentils

Enjoy this spiced favorite at weekends when you are less rushed in the morning. Brown rice and lentils combine to give you sustained energy.

Place the rice and lentils in a strainer and rinse under cold running water until the water runs clear, then put in a bowl, add cold water to cover, and let stand for 30 minutes.

Meanwhile, heat the oil in a large pan with a tight-fitting lid. Add the onion and stir for 5 minutes, or until it is softened, but not colored. Drain the rice and lentils.

Add the cumin seeds, coriander, and asafetida to the pan and cook, stirring, for 30 seconds. Add the rice and lentils and cook, stirring, for about 2 minutes, or until any excess liquid evaporates and the rice and lentils are coated in the oil.

Pour over the boiling water and stir in the salt. Return the water to a boil, stir, cover the pan, reduce the heat to low, and let simmer for 40–45 minutes, or until the rice is tender, all the liquid has been absorbed, and small holes appear all over the surface.

While the rice and lentils are cooking, place the haddock in a skillet and add water to cover. Bring to just below boiling point, reduce the heat to low, cover the skillet, and let simmer for 10–15 minutes, or until the fish flakes easily.

Drain the fish and, when it is cool enough to handle, remove all skin and bones. Flake the flesh into large chunks.

Spoon the rice and lentils onto a large serving platter and stir in the haddock flakes, eggs, and scallions. Sprinkle with the parsley and serve with some whole wheat bread.

1 eating apple, cored,
  peeled, and chopped
4$^{1}/_{2}$ oz/125 g light brown
  sugar
5$^{1}/_{2}$ oz/150 g all-purpose
  whole wheat flour
5$^{1}/_{2}$ oz/150 g all-purpose
  white flour

2 tsp baking powder
1 tbsp ground cinnamon
$^{1}/_{2}$ tsp salt
2 oz/55 g walnut halves,
  chopped
4 tbsp sunflower oil
1 large egg, beaten
8 fl oz/225 ml milk

apple muffins

Put one of these in your bag when you set off in the morning and you'll have a pick-me-up at the ready whenever your energy levels drop during the day.

Preheat the oven to 400ºF/200ºC. Lightly grease a 12-hole muffin pan.

Place the apple and half the sugar in a bowl and set aside for 5 minutes. Sift together the remaining sugar, the whole wheat flour, white flour, baking powder, cinnamon, and salt, adding in any bran remaining in the sifter. Stir in the walnuts.

In a small bowl, beat together the remaining ingredients. Stir this liquid into the dry ingredients and lightly stir together until just mixed—the mixture will be lumpy and a small amount of flour should be visible. If you over-beat the batter, the muffins will be flat.

Divide the mixture among the holes in the muffin pan, filling each hole about two-thirds full. Place the pan in the oven and bake for 20–25 minutes until the muffins are lightly browned and slightly peaked. A wooden toothpick inserted in the center should come out clean.

Remove the muffins from the oven. Turn them out immediately and place them on a cooling rack to cool. Serve warm or at room temperature.

serves 2

9 oz/250 g fresh or
  frozen blueberries
1 lb 2 oz/500 g
vanilla-flavored yogurt
$\frac{1}{2}$ large banana
lemon juice or honey,
  to taste

blueberry bliss

Enjoy this luscious smoothie all year round, as frozen blueberries have almost the same amount of nutrients, antioxidants, and fiber as fresh ones.

Put the blueberries, yogurt, and banana in a blender and blend. Add lemon juice to taste, then blend again, pour into tall glasses, and serve.

serves 2

7 oz/200 g fresh berries,
  such as raspberries
  and/or strawberries,
  hulled
1 lb 2 oz/500 g coconut-
  flavored yogurt
1/2 large banana
2 tbsp orange juice

tropical delight

Fresh berries are a powerhouse of nutrients, so a glass of this rich, creamy smoothie will get your day off to a healthy start, as well as boosting your energy levels.

Put the berries, yogurt, banana, and orange juice in a blender and blend, then pour into tall glasses and serve.

lively lunches

It can be tempting to give in to the demands of a busy day and work through lunch, but you'll find your attention and alertness failing as the afternoon wears on. From soups to salads, you'll find plenty of ideas in this chapter to boost your midday energy levels and keep you in top form throughout the afternoon.

serves 4–6

10¹/₂ oz/300 g red lentils, rinsed

4¹/₄ pints/2 liters vegetable stock or water

2 green chiles, split

1 tsp turmeric

2 tbsp sunflower oil

1¹/₂ onions, thinly sliced

2 large garlic cloves, crushed

2 tsp curry paste, mild, medium, or hot, as desired

salt and pepper

4 tbsp Greek-style yogurt and some chopped fresh cilantro leaves, to garnish

warmed naan breads, to serve

spicy red lentil soup

Lentils, great for slow-release energy, don't require soaking before cooking, making them quicker to prepare than other pulses.

Put the lentils and stock into a large pan with a tight-fitting lid. Place over high heat and slowly bring to a boil, skimming the surface as necessary. Add the chiles and turmeric, reduce the heat to very low, cover the pan, and let the lentils simmer for 25–30 minutes until they are very soft and mushy.

Meanwhile, heat the oil in another large pan over medium heat. Add the onions and garlic and fry for 5–7 minutes until the onions are tender but not brown. Add the curry paste and cook, stirring, for about a minute.

Tip the mushy lentils and any remaining water into the pan with the onions and stir together.

Put the mixture into a blender or food processor and pulse until blended. Return the mixture to the rinsed-out pan and add enough water to make a thin soup. Slowly bring to a boil. Reduce the heat, add salt and pepper to taste, and simmer for 2 minutes. If the soup is too thick, stir in extra stock, but if it is too runny, boil until the liquid reduces.

Ladle into warmed soup bowls, drizzle a tablespoon of yogurt over each, and sprinkle with chopped cilantro. Serve with the warmed naan breads.

serves 4–6

2 tbsp sunflower oil
1 onion, finely chopped
1 celery stalk, finely chopped
1 garlic clove, crushed
1.5 liters/3^{1}/$_{4}$ pints vegetable stock or water

85 g/3 oz pearl barley, rinsed
1 bouquet garni, made with 1 bay leaf, fresh thyme sprigs, and fresh parsley sprigs
2 carrots, peeled and diced

14 oz/400 g canned chopped tomatoes
pinch of sugar
^{1}/$_{2}$ head savoy cabbage, cored and shredded
salt and pepper
2 tbsp chopped fresh parsley, to garnish

chunky whole wheat bread, to serve

hearty barley-vegetable soup

The bright colors of this filling soup are an instant indication it is good for you—barley has been recognized since Roman times as a great source of energy.

Heat the oil in a large pan over medium heat. Add the onion, celery, and garlic and stir for 5–7 minutes until softened, but not browned.

Pour in the stock and bring to a boil, skimming the surface as necessary. Add the barley and bouquet garni, reduce the heat to low, cover, and simmer for 30 minutes–1 hour until the grains are just beginning to soften.

Add the carrots, tomatoes with their can juices, and the sugar and bring the liquid back to a boil. Reduce the heat to low, cover the pan, and simmer for an additional 30 minutes, or until the barley and carrots are tender.

Just before serving, remove the bouquet garni, stir in the cabbage, and add salt and pepper to taste. Continue simmering just until the cabbage wilts, then ladle into warmed bowls and sprinkle with parsley. Serve with the whole wheat bread.

serves 4–6

1¹/₂ tbsp olive oil
1 bunch scallions,
    trimmed and chopped
1 large celery stalk,
    chopped
1 garlic clove, crushed

1 starchy potato, about
    5¹/₂ oz/150 g, peeled
    and diced
1.2 liters/2¹/₂ pints
    vegetable stock
1 bay leaf

5¹/₂ oz/150 g peas
14 oz/400 g canned
    flageolets, drained and
    rinsed
salt and pepper

finely shredded fresh
    mint, to garnish
mixed-grain bread rolls,
    to serve

minty pea & bean soup

Using canned beans not only boosts the slow-release energy levels of this soup but makes it quick and easy to prepare.

Heat the oil in a large pan over medium–high heat. Add the scallions, celery, and garlic and cook, stirring, for about 3 minutes until softened. Add the potato and stir for an additional minute.

Add the stock, bay leaf, and salt and pepper to taste and bring to a boil, stirring. Reduce the heat to low, cover the pan, and simmer for 20 minutes, or until the potatoes are tender.

Add the peas and flageolets and return the soup to a boil. Reduce the heat, re-cover the pan, and continue to simmer until the peas are tender.

Remove the bay leaf, then transfer the soup to a food processor or blender and blend until smooth. Place a metal strainer over the rinsed-out pan and use a wooden spoon to push the soup through the strainer.

Add salt and pepper to taste and reheat. Ladle the soup into warmed bowls, sprinkle with mint, and serve with the bread rolls.

6 orange-fleshed sweet
potatoes, scrubbed,
rinsed, and dried
olive oil
sea salt
chopped fresh parsley,
to garnish
salad greens, to serve

Red Bell Pepper Hummus
14 oz/400 g canned
chickpeas, drained
and rinsed
2–3 tbsp fresh lemon
juice
5 tbsp tahini
2 tbsp olive oil

1 garlic clove, crushed
3½ oz/100 g charbroiled
red bell peppers in olive
oil, drained and sliced
salt and pepper

baked sweet potatoes with red bell pepper hummus

Choosing bright orange sweet potatoes rather than white potatoes for baking maintains blood sugar levels for longer—and gives you extra flavor.

Preheat the oven to 425ºF/220ºC. Use a fork to pierce the sweet potatoes all over, then rub with olive oil and sprinkle with salt.

Place the sweet potatoes directly on an oven rack and roast for 35–45 minutes until they are tender when pierced with a knife.

Meanwhile, make the Red Pepper Hummus. Put the chickpeas and 2 tablespoons of the lemon juice in a food processor and blend until a thick paste forms. Add the tahini, the olive oil, and the garlic and blend again. Add the bell peppers and salt and pepper to taste and blend again. Taste and add extra lemon juice, if desired. Scrape into a bowl, cover with plastic wrap, and chill until required.

When the potatoes are tender, slit each one lengthwise and squeeze open. Top each potato with a good spoonful of Red Pepper Hummus, sprinkle with the parsley, and serve with some salad greens.

serves 4

6 large eggs
2 tbsp chopped fresh
   basil
2 tbsp olive oil
1 small onion, sliced
2 large ripe tomatoes,
   halved, cored, and
   thinly sliced

salt and pepper
fresh arugula leaves,
   tossed with balsamic
   vinegar, olive oil, and
   sea salt, to serve

tomato frittata

Tomatoes contain a wealth of nutrients and will give your vitality a boost. They also benefit nutritionally from being cooked.

Beat the eggs in a bowl, then stir in the basil and salt and pepper to taste and set aside.

Heat 1 tablespoon of the oil in a 10-inch/25-cm nonstick skillet over medium heat. Add the onion to the skillet and fry for 5–7 minutes, until softened, but not browned.

Add the tomatoes to the skillet and fry for about 30 seconds, or until they are starting to soften. Carefully turn the onion, tomatoes, and any oil remaining in the skillet into the bowl containing the eggs.

Wipe out the skillet with paper towels. Reheat it over medium–high heat. Add the remaining oil and heat, swirling it around to coat the sides. Pour in the eggs and tomatoes and let cook for 5–6 minutes, shaking the skillet occasionally and working the set frittata into the center so the uncooked egg runs underneath.

Gently slide the frittata out of the skillet onto a large flat plate. Place the skillet upside down over the frittata, then, using an oven mitt, invert the skillet and plate, so that the uncooked side is on the bottom. Continue cooking for an additional 3–4 minutes until the frittata is set throughout.

Slide the frittata onto a plate and serve warm, or let cool and serve at room temperature. Cut into wedges and serve with the dressed arugula leaves.

small handful baby leaf
  spinach, rinsed, patted
  dry, and shredded
$1/2$ red bell pepper,
  seeded and thinly sliced
$1/2$ carrot, peeled and
  coarsely grated
4 tbsp hummus

3 oz/85 g boneless,
  skinless cooked turkey
  meat, thinly sliced
$1/2$ tbsp toasted
  sunflower seeds
1 whole wheat pita
salt and pepper

turkey salad wrap

The whole wheat pita, spinach, hummus, and sunflower seeds contribute to making this a more beneficial choice than a high-fat sandwich made with processed white bread.

Preheat the broiler to high.

Put the spinach leaves, bell pepper, carrot, and hummus into a large bowl and stir together, so all the salad ingredients are coated with the hummus. Stir in the turkey and sunflower seeds and season to taste with salt and pepper.

Put the pita under the broiler for about 1 minute on each side to warm through, but do not brown. Cut it in half to make 2 "pockets" of bread.

Divide the salad among the bread pockets and serve.

2 tbsp sunflower oil
1 onion, chopped
2 garlic cloves, crushed
7 oz/200 g buckwheat
  grains
14 oz/400 g canned
  chopped tomatoes
1/2 tsp tomato paste

pinch of sugar
9 fl oz/250 ml vegetable
  stock
1 tbsp chopped fresh
  sage, or 1/2 tbsp dried
  sage
pinch of dried chile
  flakes

115 g/4 oz feta cheese,
  drained and crumbled
salt and pepper
salad greens, to serve

buckwheat-tomato bake

Buckwheat is one of the many grains that give you a steady, slow flow of energy, rather than a quick high followed by a rapid low.

Heat the oil in a deep skillet with a tight-fitting lid over medium–high heat. Add the onion and garlic and fry for 5 minutes. Add the buckwheat grains and stir around for 1 minute until you can smell a "toasty" aroma.

Stir in the tomatoes with their can juices, the tomato paste, sugar, stock, sage, chile flakes, and salt and pepper to taste, stirring to dissolve the tomato paste. Bring to a boil, stirring, then reduce the heat to low, cover the skillet, and let simmer for 20–25 minutes until the liquid has been absorbed and the buckwheat is tender.

Lightly stir in the feta cheese, re-cover the skillet and let the buckwheat stand for up to 20 minutes. Just before serving, lightly stir with a fork. Serve with a bowl of salad greens on the side.

serves 4

1 red bell pepper, halved and seeded

4 smoked trout fillets, about 5½ oz/150 g each, skinned, any small bones removed, and flaked

4 scallions, trimmed and finely chopped

2 large chicory heads, halved, cored, and shredded

1½ tbsp Chinese rice vinegar

½ tbsp sunflower oil

2 tbsp chopped fresh parsley

salt and pepper

radicchio leaves, rinsed and dried, and some whole wheat French bread, to serve

smoked trout salad

Eat this crunchy, lowfat salad with good-quality whole wheat bread and you should feel more alert throughout the afternoon.

Run a swivel-bladed vegetable peeler along the length of the cut edges of the bell pepper to make very thin slices. Chop the slices and put them in a bowl.

Add the trout, scallions, and chicory, tossing to mix together. Add 1 tablespoon of the vinegar, the oil, parsley, and salt and pepper and toss again, then add extra vinegar as required.

Cover and chill until ready to serve. Arrange the radicchio leaves on individual plates. Toss the salad again and adjust the seasoning, if necessary. Place a portion of salad on each plate of radicchio leaves and serve with the bread.

serves 4

Dressing
125 ml/4 fl oz extra virgin olive oil
3 tbsp Chinese rice wine vinegar
1/2 tsp Dijon mustard
pinch of superfine sugar

4 large handfuls mixed salad greens, such as beet greens, escarole, endive, and radicchio
14 oz/400 g boneless, skinless cooked chicken, cut into bite-size pieces

2 satsumas, separated into segments
2 celery stalks, thinly sliced
1/2 red onion, halved and thinly sliced
2 tbsp snipped fresh chives

2 avocados
salt and pepper
2 tbsp toasted sunflower seeds, to garnish
Pita Chips (see page 92), to serve

chicken avocado salad

Add as many nutty-tasting sunflower seeds as you like to this colorful salad. Like other seeds, they are ideal energy boosters.

To make the dressing, put the oil, vinegar, mustard, sugar, and salt and pepper to taste into a small screw-top jar and shake until blended and emulsified.

Put the salad greens into a bowl, add about one third of the dressing, and lightly toss. Add the chicken, satsumas, celery, onion, chives, and the remaining dressing and toss again.

Cut the avocados in half and remove the pit, then peel away the skin. Cut the flesh into thin slices, add to the other ingredients, and gently toss together, making sure the avocado slices are completely coated with dressing so they don't discolor.

Arrange on individual plates, sprinkle with sunflower seeds, and serve with Pita Chips on the side.

serves 4–6

5 tbsp extra virgin olive oil

2 tbsp tarragon vinegar

1/2 tsp mixed grain mustard

pinch of sugar

4 oz/115 g green beans, trimmed and cut into bite-size pieces

4 oz/115 g shelled fava beans, gray outer skins removed if not young

4 oz/115 g fresh or frozen shelled peas

14 oz/400 g canned cannellini or red kidney beans, drained and rinsed

1 small red onion, thinly sliced

2 tbsp chopped fresh parsley

1 tbsp snipped fresh chives

3 oz/85 g arugula or watercress leaves

salt and pepper

Fried Provolone Cheese

olive oil

12 oz/350 g provolone cheese, cut into 12 slices

all-purpose flour, for dusting

herbed mixed bean salad with fried provolone cheese

Fried provolone cheese adds protein to this mix of beans that release their energy slowly to keep you satisfied and alert for longer.

Put the oil, vinegar, mustard, sugar, and salt and pepper to taste in a small screw-top jar and shake until blended and emulsified. Set aside.

Prepare a bowl of iced water. Bring a pan of lightly salted water to a boil. Add the green beans and fava beans and blanch for 3 minutes, or until just tender. Use a slotted spoon to remove the beans from the water and immediately transfer them to the iced water.

Return the water to a boil and blanch the peas for 3 minutes, or until tender. Remove from the water and add to the iced water to cool. Drain the beans and peas and pat dry with paper towels. Transfer to a large bowl, add the dressing, cannellini beans, onion, and herbs and toss. Cover and chill.

To make the Fried Provolone Cheese, just before you are ready to serve, heat a thin layer of oil in a large skillet over medium–high heat. Lightly dust each slice of cheese with flour, shaking off the excess. Place as many pieces as will fit in the skillet and fry for 30–60 seconds until golden brown. Flip the cheese over and continue frying until lightly browned on the other side, then remove from the skillet and keep warm while you fry the remaining pieces.

Toss the salad again, add the arugula leaves, and then add extra seasoning, if necessary. Divide the salad among individual plates and arrange the hot cheese alongside. Drizzle the cheese with olive oil, grind over some pepper, and serve.

dynamic dinners

After a busy day your energy levels will need a top-up. These easy-to-cook, vegetarian and meat-based dishes provide lean protein along with slowly digested carbohydrates to keep you going until bedtime. A good night's sleep is also important for your energy levels, so avoid caffeine, rounding off your meal with a cup of camomile tea instead.

serves 4

14 oz/400 g dried whole wheat spaghetti, linguini, or other long noodles

6 garlic cloves, crushed

1 lb 5 oz/600 g canned tuna in oil, drained, oil reserved

juice of 2 lemons

2 tbsp capers in salt, rinsed to remove the salt

finely grated rind of 2 lemons

salt and pepper

handful fresh basil leaves, to garnish

tuna pasta

When you get into the habit of choosing whole wheat pasta over the more refined varieties you'll feel revitalized throughout the day.

Bring a large pan of lightly salted water to a boil. Add the pasta and cook for 12 minutes, or according to the packet instructions, until the pasta is tender.

Meanwhile, heat all but 2 tablespoons of the reserved oil in a large deep pan over medium heat. Add the garlic and stir for 2–3 minutes until softened, but not browned. Flake the tuna and stir into the pan with the lemon juice and pepper: do not add any salt at this point. Cook, stirring, breaking up the tuna. Stir in the capers, then taste and adjust the seasoning—remember that the capers might still be salty.

Drain the pasta and add, with the remaining oil, to the pan with the tuna, using 2 forks to mix all the ingredients together. Add lemon rind to taste. Divide the pasta among serving bowls and tear basil leaves over each portion.

serves 4

10½ oz/300 g dry thin soba (buckwheat) noodles
3 tbsp sunflower or peanut oil
1 tsp dried ginger

1 tbsp Chinese rice wine vinegar
1½ tsp sesame oil
1 tsp light soy sauce
3½ oz/100 g bean sprouts
3 oz/85 g snow peas, thinly sliced

4 scallions, chopped
2 garlic cloves, crushed
1 red bell pepper, halved, seeded, and very thinly sliced
½ head cabbage, cored and thinly shredded

small handful fresh cilantro leaves
pepper
toasted sesame seeds, to garnish

wok-fried soba noodles

The crunchy bean sprouts in this recipe are packed with energy. When beans are sprouted, their overall nutritional benefits are increased.

Bring a pan of water to a boil, add the noodles, and boil for 3 minutes, or according to the packet instructions. Drain well, then add to a bowl of cold water and use your hand to swish around to remove all the starch. Drain again, then put into another bowl of cold water and set aside.

Put 2 tablespoons of the sunflower oil into a large bowl and stir in the ginger. Beat in the vinegar, sesame oil, and soy sauce. Add pepper to taste.

Drain the noodles very well, shaking off any excess water, then add to the bowl with the oil. Add the bean sprouts, snow peas, scallions, garlic, bell pepper, and cabbage and use your hands to mix together. Season to taste. If you're not cooking immediately, cover the bowl with plastic wrap and chill until 10 minutes before you want to cook.

When you're ready to cook, heat a wok over high heat until a splash of water "dances" on the surface. Add the remaining oil to the wok and heat until it shimmers.

Add the noodles and vegetables and stir-fry for 3–5 minutes until all the vegetables are hot and just tender. Add the cilantro leaves and stir them through. Taste and adjust the seasoning.

Transfer the noodles and vegetables to serving bowls and sprinkle with the sesame seeds.

serves 4

2 tbsp olive or sunflower oil

1 large chicken, cut into 8 pieces, or 8 thighs

2 large onions, sliced

2 large garlic cloves, crushed

2 tsp ground coriander

1 1/2 tsp ground ginger

1 1/2 tsp ground cumin

pinch of dried chile flakes (optional)

14 oz/400 g dried apricots, soaked overnight in 10 fl oz/ 300 ml orange juice

14 oz/400 g canned chickpeas, drained

large pinch of saffron threads

1 preserved lemon, rinsed and sliced

1 oz/30 g slivered almonds, toasted

sprigs of fresh flat-leaf parsley, to garnish

cooked couscous, to serve

chicken with apricots & chickpeas

The carbohydrate in the dried apricots and chickpeas in this spicy, slowly cooked stew, with a hint of Middle-Eastern flavorings, gives you energy.

Heat 2 tablespoons of the oil in a flameproof casserole over medium–high heat. Add as many chicken pieces as will fit without overcrowding and fry for 3–5 minutes until golden brown. Remove from the casserole and set aside while you fry the remaining pieces.

Pour off all but 2 tablespoons of the oil from the casserole. Add the onions and stir for 4 minutes. Add the garlic and continue stirring for a minute or two until the onions are softened, but not browned. Stir in the coriander, ginger, cumin and chile flakes, if using, and cook, stirring, for 1 minute.

Return the chicken pieces to the casserole with enough water to cover. Bring to a boil, then reduce the heat and let simmer for 20 minutes. Add the apricots, chickpeas, and

saffron and continue to simmer for 10 minutes, or until the chicken pieces are cooked through and the juices run clear when the meat is pierced with a skewer.

Transfer the chicken, apricots, and chickpeas to a serving platter and keep warm. Bring the liquid remaining in the casserole to a boil and reduce by half. Pour this liquid over the chicken, add the preserved lemon slices. and sprinkle with the slivered almonds. Transfer to serving plates, garnish with sprigs of parsley, and serve hot, accompanied by the couscous.

serves 4

1 oz/30 g butter
1 tbsp sunflower oil
4 large chicken breasts,
  skin removed
1 onion, chopped
1 garlic clove, crushed

2 red or green bell
  peppers, halved,
  seeded, and finely
  chopped
2 oz/55 g corn kernels,
  drained if canned,
  but straight from the
  freezer if frozen

2 oz/55 g peas
1 bay leaf, torn in half
7 fl oz/200 ml dry white
  wine
4 fl oz/125 ml quick-cook
  brown rice
9 fl oz/250 ml chicken
  stock

salt and pepper
chopped fresh parsley,
  to garnish

chicken with rice

Lean chicken is great for boosting your vitality and strength. Brown rice adds flavor and provides more slow-release energy than white rice.

Melt the butter with the oil in a large flameproof casserole over medium–high heat. Add as many chicken breasts as will fit without overcrowding the casserole and fry for 3–5 minutes until golden brown. Remove from the casserole and cook the remaining breasts, then remove those from the casserole.

Pour off all but 1 tablespoon of the oil from the casserole. Add the onion, garlic, and bell peppers and cook, stirring, for about 5 minutes until softened, but not browned. Return the chicken pieces to the casserole, add the corn, peas, and bay leaf, then add the wine and bubble until it is almost all evaporated.

Scatter the rice over the chicken pieces, making sure it rests on top of the chicken, then pour in the stock and enough water to cover all the chicken pieces. Add salt and pepper to taste.

Bring the liquid to a boil, cover the casserole, and reduce the heat to very low. Let the chicken and rice cook for 20 minutes until all the liquid has been absorbed, the rice is tender, and the chicken is cooked through.

Taste and adjust the seasoning. Scatter over the parsley and serve.

makes two 12-inch/30-cm pizzas

Pizza Dough
14 oz/400 g all-purpose whole wheat flour, plus extra for kneading
1 envelope active dry yeast
1 tsp sugar
1 tsp salt

9 fl oz/250 ml warm water
1 tbsp olive oil, plus extra for drizzling

Topping
1 lb 5 oz/600 g mixed vegetables, such as eggplants, zucchini, fennel, and bell peppers
olive oil, for brushing and drizzling

4 tbsp bottled tomato sauce
4$^{1}/_{2}$ oz/125 g rindless goat cheese, thinly sliced
sea salt and pepper, to taste

pizza with charbroiled vegetables

When you want extra energy from your diet on a daily basis, simple changes, such as using whole wheat flour rather than white flour, will set you on the right track.

To make the dough, stir the flour, yeast, sugar, and salt together in a large bowl. Make a well in the center, then stir in the warm water and the oil. Stir to make a soft dough. Turn out onto a lightly floured surface and knead until smooth and elastic. Return the dough to the rinsed bowl, drizzle with oil, then cover with plastic wrap and leave in a warm place until it has doubled in volume.

Meanwhile, prepare the vegetables. Trim the eggplants and zucchini, then cut into ¼-inch/0.5-cm slices. Cut the fronds off the fennel and slice thickly across the grain. Cut the tops off the bell peppers, then halve, seed, and cut into quarters. Heat a large, ridged cast-iron skillet over a high heat. Brush the ridges with oil. Add a batch of vegetables in a single layer and cook until they start to soften. Brush with oil and use tongs to flip the pieces over. Continue

until all the pieces are cooked through. Transfer to a plate and keep warm while you cook the remaining vegetables.

Preheat the oven to 425ºF/220ºC with 2 baking sheets inside. Turn out the dough, punch down, and knead on a lightly floured surface for 1 minute. Cut the dough in half and roll into 2 balls. Using a floured rolling pin, roll out each ball into a 12-inch/30-cm circle and place it on a hot baking sheet. Spread 2 tablespoons of the tomato sauce over each pizza base, then top with a selection of charbroiled vegetables. Sprinkle with salt and pepper and add half the cheese slices. Drizzle with oil and bake for 15 minutes, or until the bases are cooked through, the edges are golden brown, and the cheese is bubbling. Remove from the oven and serve immediately.

serves 4–6

4 fl oz/125 ml olive oil
finely grated rind and
  juice of 1 orange
1 small red onion, thinly
  sliced
1 garlic clove, very finely
  chopped
1 small red chile, seeded

and finely chopped, or
  pinch dried chile flakes
12 sprigs fresh thyme
12 small mackerel, heads
  removed, gutted,
  and rinsed inside and
  out
sea salt and pepper

chopped fresh cilantro, to
  garnish

Mediterranean Spinach
1½ tbsp olive oil, plus
  extra for brushing
1 onion
1 large garlic clove

½ tbsp ground coriander
½ tbsp ground cumin
2 lb/900 g baby leaf
  spinach, rinsed and
  shaken dry
2 oz/55 g pine nuts,
  lightly toasted
salt and pepper

broiled mackerel with mediterranean spinach

Include oily fish, such as mackerel, in your diet on a regular basis when you want to perk up your energy levels.

Put the olive oil, orange rind and juice, onion, garlic, and chile in a flat bowl large enough to hold all the mackerel and whisk until blended. Put a thyme sprig inside each mackerel, then add the fish to the marinade and use your hands to coat them.

To make the Mediterranean Spinach, heat the oil in a skillet over medium–high heat. Chop the onion, add to the skillet, and cook, stirring, for 3 minutes, then crush the garlic, add to the skillet, and continue to cook, stirring, until the onion is soft. Stir in the coriander and cumin with a pinch of salt and continue to cook, stirring, for 1 minute.

Add the spinach with just the water clinging to its leaves, using a wooden spoon to push it into the skillet, and salt

and pepper to taste. Cook, stirring, for 8 minutes, or until the leaves are wilted. Sprinkle with the pine nuts, then cover and keep warm while you broil the mackerel.

Preheat the broiler to high. Line the broiler pan with foil and lightly brush with oil. Arrange the mackerel on the pan and place the pan 4 inches/10 cm beneath the heat. Broil for 1½ minutes. Use a fish slice or metal palette knife to turn the fish. Brush with olive oil, then broil for 1½–2 minutes until the fish is cooked through and the flesh flakes easily.

Serve the mackerel accompanied by the spiced spinach.

serves 4

9 oz/250 g wild rice,
  rinsed and drained
2¹/₂ oz/75 g butter
1 tbsp olive oil, plus extra
  for greasing
14 oz/400 g white
  mushrooms, wiped and
  thinly sliced

1 tbsp chopped fresh
  tarragon, or ¹/₂ tbsp
  dried tarragon
10¹/₂ oz/300 g leeks,
  trimmed and thinly
  sliced
12 thin lemon slices

4 salmon fillets, any
  small bones removed
4 tbsp dry white
  vermouth
4¹/₂ oz/125 g sour cream
salt and pepper

baked salmon with wild rice

Look for wild rice at the supermarket. It's actually an aquatic grass and adds a delicate nutty flavor to meals.

Bring 2½ pints/1.2 liters water to a boil in a large pan. Add the rice and 1½ teaspoons of salt and return the water to the boil. Cover the pan, reduce the heat to low, and simmer for 45–50 minutes until all the liquid has been absorbed and the rice is tender. Add 1 oz/30 g of the butter and fluff with a fork.

Meanwhile, preheat the oven to 425°F/220°C. Cut out 4 circles of wax paper large enough to hold a salmon fillet with some mushrooms and leeks spooned on top. Fold the circles in half and brush the bottom halves with oil.

Melt 1 oz/30 g of the remaining butter with the oil in a large skillet over high heat. Add the mushrooms and cook, stirring, for about 6 minutes until they start to give off their liquid. Add the tarragon and salt and pepper to taste and

stir. Turn the mushrooms out of the skillet and set aside. Melt the remaining butter in the wiped-out skillet. Add the leeks with salt and pepper to taste and cook, stirring, for 6 minutes, or until tender.

Arrange 3 lemon slices in a row along the fold on each of the paper circles. Place a salmon fillet on top, top with one quarter of the mushrooms and the leeks, and add a tablespoon of vermouth, 2 tablespoons of sour cream, and some salt and pepper. Fold over the circles and crimp the edges so the parcels are sealed and none of the juices can escape. Transfer to a baking tray, place in the oven, and bake for 12 minutes or until the flesh flakes.

Serve on warmed plates, with the rice, wrapped in the paper for each diner to unwrap.

serves 4

1¹/₂ oz/45 g dried
  mushrooms
3 pints/1.4 liters boiling
  vegetable stock
2 tbsp olive oil
1 onion, chopped
2 large garlic cloves

250 g/9 oz short-grain
  brown rice
3¹/₂ fl oz/100 ml dry
  white wine
14 oz/400 g baby leaf
  spinach, rinsed and
  finely shredded

1 oz/30 g butter
2 oz/55 g Parmesan
  cheese, grated
salt and pepper

mushroom risotto

This isn't a true risotto, because it isn't creamy, but the technique is similar and it is a flavorsome way to include unrefined brown rice in your daily diet.

Put the mushrooms in a small heatproof bowl and pour over the stock, then set aside for 20 minutes, or until the mushrooms are softened. Line a strainer with muslin, place over a pan and strain the mushrooms, reserving the liquid. Set the mushrooms aside, place the stock over low heat, and bring to a simmer.

Heat the oil in a large skillet over medium–high heat. Add the onion and cook, stirring, for 3 minutes, then add the garlic and continue to cook, stirring, until the onions are softened, but not browned.

Add the rice and stir, then add the wine and let bubble until most of the liquid has evaporated. Add a ladleful of the simmering stock and stir until it is absorbed. Continue adding the stock, a ladleful at a time, until the grains are tender. Add the mushrooms.

Stir in the spinach and let cook for just a few minutes until it wilts. Add the butter and stir until it melts, then stir in the cheese. Taste and season, although you might not need much salt as the cheese is quite salty.

1 lb 10 oz/750 g fresh
   kale
2 tbsp sunflower oil
1 onion, chopped
4 large garlic cloves,
   finely chopped
2 red bell peppers,
   seeded and thinly sliced

1 large carrot, peeled
   and coarsely grated
3½ oz/100 g tiny broccoli
   florets, rinsed
pinch dried chile flakes
   (optional)
4 fl oz/125 ml vegetable
   stock

4 oz/115 g mixed fresh
   bean sprouts
handful toasted cashews,
   chopped
salt and pepper
boiled brown rice or soba
   noodles and lemon
   wedges, to serve

kale stir-fry

Quick and easy to prepare, this vegetarian dish contains a host of antioxidants and nutrients, as well as lots of fiber.

Using a sharp knife, remove any thick central cores from the kale. Stack several leaves on top of each other, then cut across them to finely shred; repeat until all the kale is shredded. Set aside.

Heat a large lidded wok or pan over high heat until a splash of water "dances" on the surface. Add the oil and swirl around. Add the onion and stir-fry for about 3 minutes, then add the garlic, bell peppers, and carrot and continue stir-frying until the onion is tender and the peppers are starting to soften.

Add the broccoli and the chile flakes, if using, and stir. Add the kale and stir. Add the stock and salt and pepper to taste, reduce the heat to medium, cover the wok, and simmer for about 5 minutes until the kale is tender.

Remove the lid and allow any excess liquid to evaporate. Use 2 forks to mix the bean sprouts through the other ingredients, then adjust the seasoning, if necessary. Serve the vegetables on a bed of rice, with some chopped cashews sprinkled over and lemon wedges on the side for squeezing over.

super snacks

Be prepared for snack attacks when your energy levels fall. While most cookies and cakes will give you a sugar rush to perk you up, not all provide a long-lasting boost. The snack and cookie recipes in this chapter include complex carbohydrates that slowly release energy into your bloodstream to keep you feeling good for longer.

makes about 14 oz/400 g

9 oz/250 g smoked
  mackerel fillets,
  skinned, any small
  bones removed, and
  flaked
4¹/₂ oz/125 g silken tofu
2 tbsp fresh lemon juice

1 tsp grated horseradish
  (optional)
1 tbsp chopped fresh dill
  or snipped fresh chives,
  plus extra for garnish
4 slices wholewheat
  bread
salt and pepper

smoked mackerel pâté with melba toast

Tofu is an excellent source of vegetarian protein, and also helps prevent blood sugar swings. In this recipe it replaces the higher-fat ingredients that are usually used.

Put the mackerel, tofu, lemon juice, and horseradish, if using, in a blender or food processor and blend until smooth. Add salt and pepper to taste, but remember that the mackerel will be quite salty.

Stir in the fresh herbs, then transfer to a bowl, cover, and chill until about 10 minutes before serving. Sprinkle over some fresh herbs.

Meanwhile, preheat the broiler to high. Toast the bread on both sides until just golden brown. Using a long, serrated knife, cut off the crusts, then thinly slice each piece of toast horizontally through the center. Cut each piece into 2 triangles, then toast the untoasted sides until they are golden and the edges have curled up. Serve with the pâté.

makes about 10 1/2 oz/300 g

14 oz/400 g canned
  cannellini beans,
  drained and rinsed
4 tbsp extra virgin olive
  oil, plus extra for
  drizzling
1 tbsp fresh lemon juice
1 garlic clove, crushed

3 oz/85 g feta cheese,
  drained
1/2 tbsp chopped fresh
  oregano, plus extra
  to garnish
3 scallions, finely
  chopped
pepper

paprika, to garnish
selection of crudités,
  such as red and yellow
  bell pepper strips,
  cucumber and carrot
  slices, and chicory
  leaves, to serve

greek-style bean & cheese dip

Canned cannellini beans are given a new twist in this energy-sustaining dip flavored with feta cheese.

Put the beans and the oil in a food processor and blend until the beans are broken up. Add the lemon juice, garlic, feta cheese, and oregano and blend again. Add pepper to taste. The dip should have a light texture, so add extra olive oil if it is too thick for dipping.

Transfer to a bowl and stir through the scallions. Cover and chill until ready to serve. Just before serving, make an indentation in the top, drizzle with olive oil, and sprinkle with oregano and paprika. Serve with a colorful selection of crudités.

3 oz/85 g dried apricots, chopped

3 oz/85 g dried cranberries

3 oz/85 g roasted cashews

3 oz/85 g shelled hazelnuts

2 oz/55 g shelled Brazil nuts, halved

2 oz/55 g flaked almonds

4 tbsp toasted pumpkin seeds

4 tbsp sunflower seeds

4 tbsp toasted pine nuts

trail mix

You don't have to be a runner or cyclist to appreciate this dried fruit, nut, and seed snack. Take a small bag with you when you leave the house in the morning to combat energy lows.

Put all the ingredients into an airtight container, close the lid, and shake several times. Shake the container before each opening, then re-seal. This mix will stay fresh for up to 2 weeks if tightly sealed after each opening.

makes 12

sunflower oil, for greasing
8 oz/225 g self-rising
  whole wheat flour
1 tsp English mustard
  powder
1 tsp salt
1 1/2 oz/40 g butter,
  chilled and finely diced

4 oz/115 g sharp cheddar
  cheese, grated
2 tbsp snipped fresh
  chives
about 5 fl oz/ 150 ml
  milk, plus a little extra
  for glazing

whole wheat cheddar scones

Biscuits are always a popular snack, and you can give them an added boost by making them with whole wheat flour, rather than the more traditional white flour.

Preheat the oven to 425ºF/220ºC. Very lightly grease a baking sheet with oil.

Put the flour, mustard powder, and salt into a food processor and pulse until blended. Add the butter and quickly pulse until crumbs form, then stir in the cheese and chives and pulse again. Slowly add just enough milk to make a soft, light dough, taking care not to over-process the dough.

Turn out the dough onto a lightly floured surface and pat out with a lightly floured rolling pin until it is about ¾ inch/2 cm thick. Handle the dough as little as possible. Use a 2-inch/5-cm round cutter to stamp out 12 biscuits, re-rolling the trimmings as necessary.

Place the scones on the baking sheet and brush the tops with milk. Bake for 10 minutes, or until risen and golden brown on top. Let cool on a cooling rack. The scones will keep for up to 2 days in an airtight container.

4$^1/_2$ oz/125 g butter, at
room temperature

7 oz/200 g superfine
sugar

1 large egg

$^1/_4$ tsp vanilla extract

4 oz/115 g all-purpose
white flour

4 oz/115 g all-purpose
whole wheat flour

$^3/_4$ tsp baking soda

pinch of salt

1$^1/_2$ oz/40 g jumbo rolled
oats

100 g/3$^1/_2$ oz raisins or
golden raisins

chewy oatmeal cookies

The oats in these sweet treats are just what you need to revive yourself when you are feeling sluggish. Have some ready when the kids come home from school.

Preheat the oven to 350ºF/180ºC.

Put the butter and sugar into a large bowl and beat until light and fluffy. Beat in the egg and vanilla extract. Sift in the white flour, whole wheat flour, baking soda, and salt, tipping in any bran left in the sifter. Add the rolled oats and raisins and stir well.

Shape the dough into 24 even-size balls and place on ungreased baking sheets. The cookies will spread during baking, so allow plenty of space between each.

Place the cookies in the oven and bake for 12–14 minutes until golden brown at the edges. Transfer to a cooling rack to cool, then store in an airtight container for up to 3 days.

makes 18

6 oz/175 g butter,
    plus extra for greasing
5½ oz/150 g dark corn
    syrup
2½ oz/70 g Demerara
    sugar
7 oz/200 g medium rolled
    oats

$2^{1}/_{2}$ oz/70 g all-purpose
    whole wheat flour
$2^{1}/_{2}$ oz/70 g raisins or
    golden raisins
finely grated rind of
    1 large orange

orange oat bars

Made with whole wheat flour and unrefined sugar, these delicious bars provide a healthy alternative to the commercial varieties.

Preheat the oven to 375ºF/180ºC. Grease a shallow 10 x 8-inch/25 x 20-cm baking pan, then line the base and sides with wax paper.

Put the butter, corn syrup, and sugar into a pan over high heat and stir until the butter and syrup have melted and the sugar has dissolved, then bring to a boil without stirring.

Put the oats, flour, raisins, and orange rind into a large heatproof mixing bowl. Pour in the butter mixture and mix all the ingredients together. Turn the mixture into the pan and use the back of a wooden spoon to spread it evenly over the base of the pan and into the corners.

Put the pan in the oven and bake for 25–30 minutes until the mixture has set. Remove from the oven, place on a cooling rack, and let cool completely.

When cool, invert the pan onto a cutting board. Lift off the pan and peel off the paper. Using a serrated knife, cut the slab in half lengthways, then cut each half into 1-inch/2.5-cm wide bars. These bars will remain fresh for up to a week wrapped in plastic wrap or stored in an airtight container.

serves 1

1 whole wheat muffin,
   split in half
extra virgin olive oil
$\frac{1}{2}$ tomato
2½ oz/70 g mixed Italian
   antipasti vegetables
   preserved in olive oil,
   drained

1 oz/30 g buffalo
   mozzarella cheese,
   drained and grated

mediterranean melts

Using a whole wheat muffin means that these open-face sandwiches give a real energy boost. For variety, try different cheeses.

Preheat the broiler to high. Place the muffin halves, cut side up, on a baking sheet under the broiler and broil for about 4 minutes, or until golden brown.

Remove the muffin halves from the heat and leave on the baking sheet: do not turn off the broiler. Brush the muffins with olive oil, then rub the tomato half over, pressing down to extract the juice. Divide the antipasti vegetables among the 2 halves, then top with the mozzarella cheese.

Return the muffin halves to the broiler and cook for 2 minutes, or until the cheese is golden and bubbling.

makes 16

2 whole wheat pitas
olive oil

pita chips

Try these a couple of times and you could lose your taste for high-fat commercial potato chips. These are good served with a dip or munched on their own.

Preheat the oven to 350ºF/180ºC. Using a serrated knife, split each pita in half, then quarter each half to make a total of 16 pieces.

Place the pieces of pita on a baking sheet, rough side up. Lightly brush each piece with olive oil, then place in the oven. Bake for 20 minutes, or until the pieces of bread are crisp and golden brown. Let cool completely before serving with dips or salads, or using as a snack. These chips will keep fresh in an airtight container for up to 3 days.

serves 4–6

1 eggplant
2 tbsp olive oil
1 onion, chopped
2 large garlic cloves,
    finely chopped
$\frac{1}{2}$ tbsp ground cumin
1 tsp ground coriander

14 oz/400 g canned
    chopped tomatoes
1 tbsp fresh lemon juice
dried chile flakes, to
    taste (optional)
3 tbsp finely chopped
    fresh mint

salt and pepper
sprigs of fresh mint, to
    garnish
Pita Chips (see page 92)
    or wholewheat pitas,
    lightly toasted, to serve

eggplant caviar

This Mediterranean-inspired dip is packed with flavors. Baking the eggplant, rather than frying it, keeps the overall fat content low.

Preheat the oven to 450ºF/230ºC. Prick the eggplant all over with a fork, place on a baking sheet and roast for 40 minutes, or until it collapses. When it is cool enough to handle, scrape the flesh into a bowl and discard the skin.

Meanwhile, heat the oil in a large skillet over medium–high heat. Add the onion and cook, stirring, for 3 minutes, then add the garlic, cumin, and coriander and stir for an additional 2 minutes, or until the onions are soft.

Stir in the eggplant flesh and the tomatoes with their can juices. Add the lemon juice, chile flakes, if using, and salt and pepper to taste. Bring to a low boil and leave to bubble for 5–10 minutes, stirring occasionally, until much of the liquid has evaporated and the flavors are blended.

Leave to cool, then stir in the mint and adjust the seasoning, if necessary. Garnish with sprigs of fresh mint and serve with the Pita Chips.